Sewing for
CHRISTMAS

Sewing for CHRISTMAS

Rebecca McCallion

NEW HOLLAND

Dedication

To the love of my life, Stefan, for his unending support.
To Eli and Scarlett for their valuable thoughts and suggestions.

CONTENTS

INTRODUCTION

Welcome to my debut book! I am so excited to be able to share my projects with you and I hope that they will inspire you to create your own handmade Christmas this year.

As you will see, I love to design and make sweet, adorable and feminine projects. I'm looking forward to decorating my home with these projects this Christmas to create a cheerful and festive look. You can add your own style to each one to create a unique look just for you. Almost all of these items are quick to make, especially the decorations, which can be stitched entirely by hand. With just a small amount of festive fabric, you could create a whole new look for your Christmas tree. There's plenty of projects to choose from, including ideas for gift bags, a hessian Christmas sack, a festive cushion and a Christmas tree skirt. There's even a super cute pet idea to get your four-legged friends involved in the festive cheer this year.

I've included different techniques throughout the 20 projects because the more techniques you know, the more things you can create. One simple technique can open up a world of ideas for you and inspire your creations. If there's something mentioned that you would like to know more about, check out the video tutorials on my YouTube channel for full instructions. If you have any questions regarding the patterns and templates in this book, please contact me on Facebook or at sewingforchristmas@gmail.com.

I hope you have fun making your Christmas projects this year, and I wish you a very happy Christmas.

Bec xx

Facebook: https://www.facebook.com/rebeccalmccallion
YouTube: Rebecca McCallion
Etsy: www.lovegrowcreate.etsy.com

PATTERNS

CHRISTMAS STOCKING

Christmas just isn't Christmas without a festive stocking hanging from the mantelpiece (or wherever suits).

SHOPPING LIST

* 40 x 60 cm (16 x 24 in) white felt, for the stocking
* 40 x 25 cm (16 x 10 in) red cotton fabric, for the cuff
* Red embroidery thread
* 50 cm (20 in) of 2.5 cm (1 in) wide white organza ribbon, for the trim
* 40 cm (16 in) of 4 cm (1½ in) wide red organza ribbon, for the trim
* 3 cm (1¼ in) red button
* Matching sewing thread

ESSENTIALS

* A3 printer/photocopier
* Tracing paper
* Pencil
* Fabric scissors
* Pins
* Sewing machine
* Hand-sewing needle
* Iron and ironing board
* Paper scissors

PREPARE ME

1 Photocopy the stocking template provided to the required size. Photocopy or trace the flower template provided. Cut out the paper templates.

2 From white felt, cut 2 stocking pieces and 1 flower.

3 From red cotton fabric, cut 1 piece 32.5 x 22.5 cm (13 x 9 in) for the stocking cuff. Cut 1 piece 16 x 4 cm (6¼ x 1½ in) for the hanging loop.

MAKE ME

All seam allowances are 5 mm (¼ in).

1   Place the white felt stocking pieces right sides together. Pin and stitch around all edges, except for the top edge. Stay stitch (work running stitch) around the top edge. Turn the stocking right side out.

2   To make the cuff, with right sides together, sew the short ends of the cuff piece together to form a tube. Press open the seam. Fold it in half lengthwise with wrong sides together. Place inside the stocking, matching the raw edges with the top edge of the stocking. Pin in place.

3   To make the hanging loop, fold the fabric in half lengthwise, wrong sides together, and press. Unfold. Fold the long raw edges in to the centre crease. Press. Refold the original crease lengthwise, enclosing the long raw edges and press. Sew the folded edges together, stitching close to the fold. Form into a loop. Insert the loop between the cuff and stocking at the centre back seam, aligning all raw edges.

4   Sew the cuff in place by stitching around the top edge of the stocking. Turn the cuff into place over the top raw edge of the stocking. The loop should now be in the correct position for hanging. Press in place.

DECORATE ME

1   Tie the white organza ribbon into a bow and cut the ends on the diagonal.

2   Twist the centre of the red ribbon once and match the twist to the centre of the ribbon bow.

3   Arrange the bow, twisted red ribbon, white felt flower and button on the cuff (see photograph for placement). Thread the red embroidery thread through a large needle and tie a knot at the ends. Position the button so that it is centred on the flower motif, then stitch it in place using the threaded needle and catch all the other decorations in the stitching, so that they are held securely.

TIPS

Felt tends to stretch when it is handled a lot and will not regain its original shape. Stay stitching will help with this.

Omit the flower decoration for a more masculine stocking.

Hide some small treats inside the stocking to make Christmas extra special for a loved one.

FESTIVE BUNTING

Bunting adds such a lovely touch to a room. The instructions here are to make a length with seven flags, but once you know how to make it, you can make it to any length.

SHOPPING LIST

* 70 x 20 cm (28 x 8 in) red stripe cotton fabric
* 70 x 20 cm (28 x 8 in) red snowflake cotton fabric
* 50 x 20 cm (20 in x 8 in) red polka dot cotton fabric
* 10 x 110 cm (4 x 44 in) plain red cotton fabric, for the binding
* Red sewing thread

ESSENTIALS

* Tracing paper or template plastic (optional)
* Pencil (optional)
* A4 printer/photocopier (optional)
* Card (card stock)
* Paper scissors
* Sewing machine
* Iron and ironing board
* Fabric scissors
* Glue
* Pins

PREPARE ME

1 Trace or photocopy the basic bunting template provided. Glue the copy to a piece of card (card stock) and cut out.

2 Using the template as a guide, draw 6 triangles on the stripe fabric, 4 on the snowflake fabric and 4 on the polka dot fabric. Cut each out.

3 Cut the plain red cotton fabric in half to make two strips, each 5 x 110 cm (2 x 44 in).

MAKE ME

All seam allowances are 5 mm (¼ in).

1   Pair up triangles of matching fabric. Arrange the pairs right sides together, and sew together along the long edges. Clip the seam allowance at the point. Turn right side out and use the tip of the scissors to carefully push out the point. Press.

2   For the binding strip, join the plain red strips, right sides together, at one short end to create one long length. Press the seam open. Turn in 1 cm (⅜ in) at each short end and press. Fold the strip in half lengthwise and press. Open out the fabric and then turn the long raw edges in to the centre fold. Press in place. Fold in half again on the original fold to enclose the raw edges.

3   Mark the centre of the binding strip with a pin. Insert the raw edges of one triangle between the folds of the binding, aligning the centre of the raw edge with the pin on the binding. Pin another triangle to each side of the first one so that the triangles touch at the top corners inside the folded binding. Pin in place. Continue to insert and pin triangles to the right and left of these triangles until all are in position.

4   Sew along the whole length of the red binding along the edge where folds meet, catching each triangle along the way.

NOEL BUNTING

Here are a few extra techniques to add decoration and a personal touch to bunting.

SHOPPING LIST

* 30 x 110 cm (12 x 44 in) white floral print cotton, for the flags
* 35 x 110 cm (14 x 44 in) white cotton fabric, for the flags and binding
* 15 x 110 cm (6 x 44 in) gold/brown cotton fabric, for the letters and flowers
* 15 x 40 cm (4 x 16 in) paper-backed fusible webbing, for the appliqué
* 3.5 x 97 cm (1½ x 38 in) cream cotton for the flowers
* 4 cream organza ribbons, each 1.25 x 25 cm (½ x 10 in), for the bows
* 2 large cream buttons
* 5 small cream flower buttons
* Matching sewing thread
* Small piece of hessian (burlap), for the flower centres

ESSENTIALS

* Sewing machine
* Iron and ironing board
* Hand-sewing needle
* Fabric scissors
* Paper scissors
* A4 printer/photocopier (optional)
* Tracing paper or template plastic (optional)
* Pencil (optional)
* Craft glue
* Card (card stock)
* Baking paper
* Pins

PREPARE ME

1   Trace or photocopy the noel bunting template provided and the noel letters. Glue the tracings to card and cut out adding 5 mm (¼ in) seam allowance on all sides.

2   From the white cotton fabric, cut 2 strips of binding, each 6 x 110 cm (2½ x 44 in).

3   Using the bunting template, draw 6 triangles on the white floral print cotton and 6 on the remaining white cotton fabric.

4   Protecting the iron and ironing board with baking paper. Following the manufacturer's instructions, press the fusible webbing to the wrong side of one end of the gold/brown fabric. Allow to cool. Place the letter templates on the paper side of the fusible webbing, reversing the way in which the letters read. Cut out the letters on the drawn line.

5   From the remaining gold/brown fabric, cut 2 strips, each 5 x 48 cm (2 x 19 in), for the flowers.

6   Cut the cream cotton strip, for the flowers, in half to yield 2 lengths, each 3.5 x 48 cm (1½ x 19 in).

7   From hessian, roughly cut 2 flowers, each 4 cm (1½ in) wide.

8   Make 4 bows from the organza ribbons.

MAKE ME

All seam allowances are 5mm (¼ in).

1   Peel off the paper backing from the appliqué letters. Arrange each, fusible webbing side down, on the right side of four of the white floral triangles, placing them 3.75 cm (1½ in) from the top. Press to fuse in place, protecting the iron and ironing board as before.

2   Set the sewing machine to a buttonhole stitch and appliqué each letter to its background, ensuring the stitching covers the raw edge of the letter.

3   Pair up the triangles so that each pair is made up of one floral print triangle and one plain white triangle. Sew each pair together along the long angled edges. Clip the seam at the point. Turn right side out, using the point of the scissors to push out the tip. Press.

4   Join the white binding strips together at one short end to create one long length and press the seam open. Turn in 1 cm (⅜ in) at each short ends and press.

5   Fold the binding in half lengthwise, with wrong sides together, and press. Open out the fold. Turn in the long raw edges to the centre crease. Press. Fold in half to enclose the raw edges.

6   Pin-mark the centre of the strip and insert the raw edges of the 'O' triangle to the left of this marker, placing the raw edges of the flag inside the binding. Place the 'E' triangle to the right of this marker, arranging each so there is 2 cm (¾ in) of space between them. Pin. Add the 'N' and 'L' triangles, then place a plain triangle at each end. Sew along the length

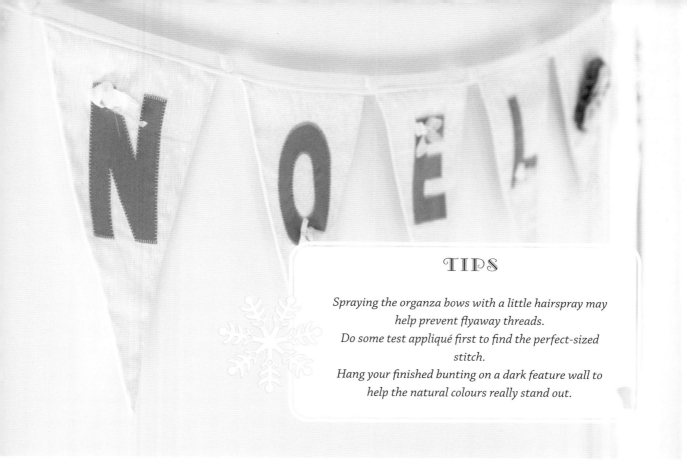

TIPS

Spraying the organza bows with a little hairspray may help prevent flyaway threads.
Do some test appliqué first to find the perfect-sized stitch.
Hang your finished bunting on a dark feature wall to help the natural colours really stand out.

of the binding close to the edge where the folded edges meet, catching in each triangle along the way.

DECORATE ME

1   Sew one small flower button between each flag on the binding strip.

2   Hand stitch the 4 bows to the letters using the photograph as a guide, catching the front triangle only so the stitching is not seen on the back of the bunting.

3   To make the flowers, take each 5 x 48 cm (2 x 19 in) length of gold/brown cotton and work a running stitch 3 mm (⅛ in) in from one long edge of each. Leaving a long tail at each end. Pull the thread tight to gather the fabric. Stitch the short ends together with a 5 mm (¼ in) seam to create a ruffled circle, ensuring the centre gap is as small as possible. Repeat with the cream fabric.

4   Arrange each gold/brown ruffled circle in the centre of one of the undecorated triangles. Arrange the cream ruffled circle on top. Put one hessian flower on top, then a large button and hand stitch decoration to the front triangle only.

FESTIVE HAND TOWEL

Sometimes projects just have to be made, even if they're not the most practical. Buttons might not be conducive to drying your hands, but they certainly look lovely!

SHOPPING LIST

* 1 white hand towel
* Pink ribbon, 3 mm (⅛ in) wide, to fit the width of the hand towel, twice, plus seam allowances, plus an extra 20 cm (8 in) length
* Green trim, 5 mm (¼ in) wide, to fit the width of the hand towel, twice, plus seam allowances
* Pink polka dot ribbon, 2.5 cm (1 in) wide, to fit the width of the hand towel, twice, plus seam allowances
* Assorted pink buttons

* Green ric-rac braid, 5 mm (¼ in) wide, for the Christmas tree decoration
* 2 cm (¾ in) of green and pink trim, for the tree trunk
* Matching sewing thread

ESSENTIALS

* Fabric scissors
* Hand-sewing needle

PREPARE ME

1 Cut the pink ribbon into two equal halves. Repeat with the green trim, and the polka dot ribbon. Sew the ribbons and trim to each end of the hand towel, turning in a small seam allowance at each raw end of the ribbon or trim and using the photograph as a guide for placement.

2 To make the Christmas tree, place a row of 5 large buttons for the bottom of the tree on the hand towel, and just above the ribbon trim. Centre the buttons along the width of the hand towel. Cut a piece of green ric-rac braid slightly longer than the button row and place below the buttons. Cut another piece of ric-rac braid to the length of the button row and place above

the buttons. Place 4 medium buttons in a row above the ric-rac braid and centred above the row just placed.

3   Cut a length of ric-rac braid to the length of this row and place above the row. Place 3 smaller buttons above the ric-rac braid and centred above the row just placed.

4   Cut a length of ric-rac braid to the length of this row and place above the row. Place 2 small buttons above the ric-rac braid and centred above the row just placed.

5   Cut a piece of green ric-rac braid to the length of these two buttons and place above the row. Place 1 shiny button above the ric-rac braid and centred above the row just place.

MAKE ME

1   Remove all the buttons and ric-rac braid from the hand towel, and set them aside in the same shape as they were placed on the hand towel. Hand stitch the buttons in place, one at a time, leaving space for the ric-rac braid below as well as the green and pink trim for the tree trunk. Sew the ric-rac braid above and below the bottom row of buttons.

2   Continue to attach buttons and ric-rac braid until the tree is complete.

DECORATE ME

1   Tie the 20 cm (8 in) length of 3 mm (⅛ in) pink ribbon into a small bow. Hand stitch it to the top of the tree.

2   Cut a small piece of pink and green trim and sew between the base of the tree and the top of the ribbon trim to create the tree trunk.

TIPS

Make a set of hand towels by using different ribbons, colours or shapes. Hand towels with a heavily woven strip at each end are perfect for this project, as the pink polka dot ribbon can be place in this space. Decorate your kitchen or bathroom with your new hand towel.

TIPS

The dot on the 'i' of 'Celebrations' will be separate, so it is best to leave it uncut until you are ready to glue it to the wine bag.

Try making your own 'Celebrations' template in your own hand writing to add a personal touch.

It's best to use a warm bottle of wine because cold wine creates condensation on the outside of the bottle, which will wet the wine bag.

This wine bag provides a snug fit to an average size wine bottle (24 cm/9½ in diameter). For a larger bottle, or a looser fit, add the desired measurement to the width of the bag pieces, lining pieces and red fabric piece.

CELEBRATIONS WINE BAG

This festive bag is a great way to present a gift of wine to a friend at Christmas time.

SHOPPING LIST

* 30 x 40 cm (12 x 16 in) white and silver cotton fabric, for the bag outer
* 30 x 40 cm (12 x 16 in) white cotton fabric, for the lining
* 6.5 x 28 cm (2½ x 11½ in) red cotton fabric, for the label
* Scrap of white felt, for the letters
* 60 cm (24 in) length of 4 cm (1½ in) wide red organza ribbon

ESSENTIALS

* Sewing machine
* Iron and ironing board
* Fabric scissors
* Tracing paper
* Fabric marker (optional)
* Pencil
* Pen (optional)
* Black medium permanent marker
* Craft glue
* Pins

PREPARE ME

1 Trace the 'celebrations' template provided, then go over the tracing with the black medium permanent marker. Put the tracing over a light source (such as a tablet or computer screen), then tape the scrap of white felt on top. Trace over the letters using a pen or pencil, then cut out carefully.

2 Using craft glue, stick the letters to the middle of the red cotton fabric for the label, on the right side.

Leave to dry. Turn in 5 mm (¼ in) on the long edges of the label fabric to the wrong side and press.

3 From the white and silver cotton, cut 2 pieces, 15 cm (6 in) x 40 cm (16 in), for the bag outer.

4 From the white fabric, cut 2 pieces, 15 cm (6 in) x 40 cm (16 in), for the bag lining.

MAKE ME

All seam allowances are 5 mm (¼ in).

1   Put the white cotton lining pieces right sides together and sew around the long edges and one short end, leaving a 4 cm (1½ in) gap in one long side for turning.

2   To create a bag base, splay out the fabric at one side seam so that the seam is aligned with that of the bag base seam and you have a pointed corner. Measure 2 cm (¾ in) from the corner along the side seam. Draw a line perpendicular to the seam at this point. Pin. Sew along the drawn line and cut away the excess seam. Repeat on the other corner.

3   Place the white and silver fabric outer pieces right sides together and sew along one long side only. Open out and press the seam open.

4   Arrange the red fabric label right side up on the right side of the bag outer, aligning raw edges and with pressed edges folded under. The red label sits 5.5 cm (2¼ in) from the bag bottom. Pin in place. Top stitch along both long folded edges.

5   Fold the bag outer lengthwise with right sides together and sew along the bag bottom and remaining long side. Create a bag base as for the lining.

6   Place the bag outer inside the bag lining, with right sides together and raw edges aligned. Sew around the top edge.

7   Turn the bag through the gap in the lining. Close the gap in the lining using ladder stitch and push the lining into the bag. Press. Top stitch around the top of the bag.

DECORATE ME

1   Place a bottle of wine inside the bag.

2   Tie red ribbon around the top of the bag over the wine bottle neck.

3   Trim the ribbon ends on an angle, as desired.

TINY CHRISTMAS TREE STOCKING

This tiny stocking is so adorable. Why not make a few to hang on your Christmas tree?

SHOPPING LIST

* Red felt scraps, for the stocking
* White felt scraps, for the cuff
* 1 small red button
* 10 cm (4 in) of 1 cm (⅜ in) wide red and white ribbon, for hanging
* Matching sewing thread

ESSENTIALS

* Sewing machine
* Iron and ironing board
* Fabric scissors
* Craft glue
* A4 printer/photocopier (optional)
* Tracing paper or template plastic (optional)
* Pencil (optional)
* Needle
* Paper scissors

PREPARE ME

1 Trace or photocopy the small stocking, small star and dot templates and cut out.

2 From red felt, cut 2 stockings and 2 dots.

3 From white felt, cut 1 star and 2 stocking cuffs. Add a seam allowance to the top of the cuff when you cut it out.

4 Sew the red button to the middle of the white felt star.

MAKE ME

All seam allowances are 5 mm (¼ in).

1 Place the stocking pieces together, matching all edges, and stitch around the outline leaving the top open. Turn right side out carefully to avoid distorting the felt shape.

2 Place the cuffs together, matching all edges, and sew the side edges together. Place the cuff inside the top of the stocking, aligning raw edges.

3 Match the short ends of the ribbon to create a hanging loop. With raw edges aligned, place the loop inside the stocking and between the stocking and cuff at the back seam.

4 Sew around the top of the stocking, catching the hanging loop, then turn out the cuff to the right side. Press.

DECORATE ME

1 Glue the star to one side of the stocking.

2 Glue the two dots to the cuff near the side seam.

3 Make 2 stitches inside the dots to make them look like tiny buttons.

TIPS

To avoid losing the small red dots, cut them out just before you glue them to the stocking.
Felt has a tendency to stretch when handled and does not regain its original shape. If you're worried about stretching the top of the stocking, try stay stitching around the top first.
Make one for each family member and put a tiny treat inside for Christmas Eve.

CHRISTMAS TREE HEART

Decorate your Christmas tree with some of these sweet hearts.

SHOPPING LIST

* Red felt scraps
* Cream open-weave fabric scraps
* Length of thin cream cord, for hanging
* 1 small red button
* 2 small bells
* Cream embroidery thread
* Toy stuffing

ESSENTIALS

* Fabric scissors
* Large hand-sewing needle
* A4 printer/photocopier
* Tracing paper
* Pencil
* Paper scissors

PREPARE ME

1 Trace or photocopy the heart and small star templates provided and cut out.

2 From red felt scraps, cut 2 hearts.

3 From cream open-weave fabric, cut 1 star.

MAKE ME

1 Hand stitch the edges of the heart shapes together using cream embroidery thread and whip stitch, and leaving a 3 cm (1¼ in) opening on one straight side for stuffing.

2 Thread the cord through a needle. Take the cord through the centre top of the heart on each side of the centre stitch. Pull the cord ends to the gap in the heart, trim so the hanging loop is the desired length

and knot the ends. Pull the loop up so that the knot is just inside the top of the heart.

3   Stuff the heart firmly with toy stuffing. Whip stitch the opening closed.

DECORATE ME

1   Embroider 4 stars on the left-hand side of the heart.

2   Arrange the open-weave star on the right-hand side of the heart and place a red button in the centre. Stitch in place, leaving a tail of embroidery thread hanging at each end.

3   Tie a bell to the end of each tail and trim the ends.

TIPS

Try to make each stitch around the outside of the heart as even as possible, but don't aim for perfection because the beauty of hand stitching is its handmade look.
You can decorate the front of the heart before stitching the two halves together if you prefer; however, it's easier to find the right placement for decorative stitches once the heart is stuffed.
Make as many as you like to decorate your tree.

CHRISTMAS TREE STAR

Add some lovely decorative stars to your tree for a gorgeous personal touch.

SHOPPING LIST

* White felt scraps
* Cream open-weave fabric scraps
* Bronze chiffon scrap
* 1 medium red button
* Red embroidery thread
* White embroidery thread
* Toy stuffing

ESSENTIALS

* Fabric scissors
* Large hand-sewing needle
* A4 printer/photocopier
* Tracing paper
* Pencil
* Paper scissors

PREPARE ME

1   Trace or photocopy the Christmas tree star template (provided at full size) and cut out.

2   From the white felt, cut 2 stars.

3   From the cream open-weave fabric, cut 1 star and then reduce the size all round by 5 mm (¼ in).

4   From bronze chiffon, cut a circle that is 5 mm (¼ in) larger than the button. Scallop the edges of the circle so it looks more like a flower.

5   Cut a 10 cm (4 in) length of red embroidery thread for the hanging loop.

MAKE ME

1   Hand stitch the edges of the felt star shapes together using blanket stitch. Leave a 3 cm (1¼ in) opening at one inner corner for stuffing.

2   Thread the 10 cm (4 in) piece of red embroidery thread through the top point of the star (on each side of the centre stitch). Pull the ends to the gap in the side and tie a knot. Pull the loop so that the knot is just inside the top of the star.

3   Stuff the star firmly with toy stuffing. Blanket stitch the opening closed.

DECORATE ME

The decorations are stitched to the front felt star only. Do not stitch all the way through to the back felt star.

1   Centre the open-weave star on the stuffed star. Place the chiffon flower in the centre and the red button on top.

2   Using red embroidery thread, hand stitch the button and flower to the stuffed star.

3   Using white embroidery thread, stitch some stems and leaves along each point of the star, catching the open-weave and front felt stars only and leaving room at the points for red roses.

4   Using red embroidery thread, stitch a red rose at each point of the star, catching the open-weave and front felt stars only.

TIPS

Try to make each stitch around the outside of the star as even as possible for neatness, but don't aim for perfection because the beauty of hand stitching is its handmade look.

Repeat the Decorate Me steps on the other side of the star for a double-sided decoration.

It's best not to tie off the thread for the outside stitching until after the decoration is stuffed and the opening closed.

CHRISTMAS TREE REINDEER

Tree decorations don't get much more adorable than this tiny reindeer. Why not make a bigger version for a wall decoration or bunting?

SHOPPING LIST

* Light brown felt scraps
* Dark brown felt scraps
* Red felt scraps
* White felt scraps
* Black felt scraps
* 1 red polka dot button
* 1 small bell
* 10 cm (4 in) of 1 cm (⅜ in) wide red and white ribbon
* Red embroidery thread
* Cream embroidery thread
* Red sewing thread
* Toy stuffing

ESSENTIALS

* Fabric scissors
* Large hand-sewing needle
* Craft glue
* A4 printer/photocopier
* Tracing paper
* Pencil
* Paper scissors

PREPARE ME

1 Trace or photocopy the reindeer and small heart templates provided and cut out.

2 From the light brown felt, cut 2 reindeers, minus the antlers.

3 From dark brown felt, cut 2 antlers, adding 5 mm (¼ in) at the bottom edge only. Cut 2 hooves to fit the bottom of the reindeer's legs.

4 From the red felt, cut 1 small heart.

5   From white felt, cut an oval eye.

6   From black felt, cut a small dot for the pupil.

7   Cut a 10 cm (4 in) length of red embroidery thread for the hanging loop.

MAKE ME

1   Glue the ends of the antlers in place on the reindeer's head. Glue the hooves on the reindeer's legs. Leave to dry.

2   Hand stitch the reindeer pieces together using running stitch, 3 mm (⅛ in) from the raw edge, making sure to catch the antlers and hooves in the stitching and leave the stomach open for stuffing.

3   Thread the 10 cm (4 in) piece of red embroidery thread through the inner point of the reindeer's neck (on each side of a stitch). Pull the ends inside to the gap in the stomach and tie a knot. Pull the loop up so that the knot is just inside the top of the reindeer.

4   Stuff the reindeer firmly with toy stuffing.

5   Use running stitch to close the stomach opening.

DECORATE ME

1   Glue the small heart near to the reindeer's tail. Whip stitch around the edges of the heart, catching the heart and front reindeer piece only (do not stitch through to the back of the reindeer).

2   Glue the eye to the head and the black dot pupil to the eye.

3   Wrap the ribbon around the reindeer's neck and use red sewing thread to stitch in place at the back of the neck. Cut the ribbon ends to length.

4   Use red sewing thread to attach the small bell to the centre front of the ribbon and to attach the button to the end of the nose.

TIPS

Try to make each stitch around the outside of the reindeer as even as possible, but don't aim for perfection because the beauty of hand stitching is its handmade look.
It's best not to tie off the thread for the outside stitching until after the decoration is stuffed and the opening closed.
Make as many as you like to decorate your tree.

HESSIAN CHRISTMAS SACK

The hessian used for this Santa sack gives it a lovely rustic look. Feel like a real-life Santa this Christmas by delivering a Santa sack full of gifts

SHOPPING LIST

* 126 x 50 cm (50 x 20 in) hessian (burlap), for the sack
* 126 x 75 cm (50 x 30 in) large polka dot fabric in red, for the bag lining and flap
* 112 x 22 cm (44 x 9 in) red chiffon, for the bow
* Red felt scraps, for the heart
* Cream open-weave scraps, for the heart
* Red embroidery thread
* White embroidery thread
* 30 cm (12 in) of 1 cm (⅜ in) wide red satin ribbon
* 1.5 m (60 in) thin cream cord
* 2 medium silver bells
* Red sewing thread

ESSENTIALS

* Sewing machine
* Iron and ironing board
* Fabric scissors
* Large hand-sewing needle
* 2 safety pins
* A4 printer/photocopier
* Tracing paper
* Pencil
* Paper scissors

PREPARE ME

1   Trace or photocopy the large and small heart templates provided and cut out.

2   From the red felt, cut 2 large hearts.

3   From the cream open-weave fabric, cut 2 small hearts.

4   From polka dot fabric, for the bag lining, cut 1

piece, 126 x 50 cm (50 x 20 in). Cut 1 flap, 126 x 22 cm (50 x 9 in).

5   Cut 3 lengths of thin cream cord, each 30 cm (12 in). Tie the lengths together at one end and attach to something sturdy with a safety pin. Plait (braid) the three lengths. Secure the end with a safety pin and unpin the knotted end.

6   Tie the 2 bells to the centre of the remaining piece of cord.

MAKE ME

All seam allowances are 1 cm (⅜ in).

1   Fold the hessian sack outer in half, with right sides together, so that the short ends meet. Sew both long edges. Turn right side out.

2   Fold the polka dot lining in half, with right sides together, so that the short ends meet. Sew both long edges, leaving an 8 cm (3¼ in) gap on one edge for turning through.

3   Fold the polka dot flap in half, right sides together, so that the short ends meet. Sew the short edge. Press open the seam. Fold in half lengthwise with wrong sides together.

4   Place the hessian sack inside the lining so that right sides are facing and raw edges and seams are matching. Place the folded flap between the sack and the lining with raw edges and seams matching. Sew around the top of the sack, then turn right side out through the gap in the lining. Close the gap in the

lining using ladder stitch. Push the lining into the sack and fold the flap over the sack outer. Press.

DECORATE ME

1   Place the large hearts together and insert one end of the plaited cord between the layers at the centre top. The entire plaited cord should be inside. Sew around the edges of the heart, leaving a gap for turning at one side. Turn right side out carefully so as not to stretch the opening. The cord should now be outside the heart. Stuff the heart firmly and close the opening using ladder stitch.

2   Embroider 'Christmas' (with a line and cross underneath) to the front of the heart.

3   Repeat to make the small heart, using the red ribbon in place of the plaited cord. Stay stitch at the opening to avoid fraying. Embroider the word 'Merry' on the heart.

4   Cut the other end of the red ribbon so that it is 4 cm (1½ in) shorter than the plaited cord and cut the thin cream cord shorter still.

5   Attach the other end of the ribbon, plaited cord and both ends of the thin cord to the underside of the flap at the centre front of the sack. Stitch through the back of the flap only so the stitches do not show on the right side.

6   Fold the chiffon in half lengthwise and sew along the long edge where the raw edges meet. Turn right side out and press carefully so as not to melt the chiffon. Tie the chiffon into a big bow. Attach the bow to the centre front of the flap. Place a few stitches at the top of the bow loops to ensure the bow doesn't droop. Cut the ends on a diagonal at the desired length.

TIPS

Embroider both sides of the hearts to create double-sided decorations.
Omit the decorations for a more masculine Santa sack.

TIPS

Add length to the fabric, ribbon, cord and elastic for a larger scrunchie. You will also need more bells.
Tie your scrunchie around a bun or pony tail to add a finishing touch to your Christmas outfit.

FESTIVE SCRUNCHIE

Look the part on Christmas day with this festive scrunchie.

SHOPPING LIST

* 45 x 10 cm (18 x 4 in) red polka dot fabric
* 23 cm (9 in) of 1 cm (⅜ in) wide elastic
* 45 cm (18 in) of 5 mm (¼ in) wide red satin ribbon
* 45 cm (18 in) of thin cream cord
* 14 small bells
* Red sewing thread

ESSENTIALS

* Sewing machine
* Iron and ironing board
* Fabric scissors
* Hand-sewing needle
* 1 safety pin
* Pliers or similar tool for clamping

PREPARE ME

1 Thread the bells onto the cord and clamp them in place 3 cm (1¼ in) apart.

2 Centre the ribbon along the length of the polka dot fabric and stitch in place.

3 Hand stitch the cord to the ribbon at each end and in between each bell.

MAKE ME

All seam allowances are 5 mm (¼ in).

1 Fold the polka dot fabric in half lengthwise and with right sides together. Sew the long raw edge together. Turn through and press.

2 Attach one end of the elastic to the safety pin. Thread the elastic through the scrunchie, safety pin end first, so both ends are visible. Tie the elastic ends together. Turn in the raw edges of the scrunchie by 5 mm (¼ in). Ladder stitch the ends together all around.

GINGHAM CHRISTMAS TABLE RUNNER

Serve up a tasty Christmas feast on this country-style table runner.

SHOPPING LIST

* 37 cm x 1.5 m (15 x 60 in) gingham, for the tablecloth
* 37 x 50 cm (15 x 20 in) white cotton fabric, for the tablecloth
* 11 x 70 cm (4½ x 30 in) red cotton fabric, for the yo-yos
* 3 m (3¼ yd) of 5 mm (¼ in) wide red satin ribbon
* 37 cm x 2 m (15 x 79 in) calico, for the lining
* 6 gingham buttons
* Red sewing thread

ESSENTIALS

* Sewing machine
* Iron and ironing board
* Fabric scissors
* Hand-sewing needle
* A4 printer/photocopier
* Tracing paper
* Pencil
* Paper scissors
* Craft glue
* Thin card (card stock)

PREPARE ME

1 Trace or photocopy the circle template. Glue the copy to thin card (card stock) and cut out. Use the template to cut 6 circles from red cotton fabric. Turn in a small seam around the edge of each circle, and hold in place with running stitch, working the stitching close to the folded edge. Pull the thread to gather the edges of the circle into a yo-yo. Secure by tying off the end of the thread. Sew a button to the centre of each yo-yo.

2 Fold the gingham for the tablecloth in half so that short ends meet. Cut along the fold. Fold each half in half again so that the short ends meet. Cut along the fold.

3 From the white cotton fabric for the tablecloth, cut 3 pieces, each 37 x 9 cm (15 x 3½ in). Cut 2 pieces, each 37 x 16 cm (15 x 6¼ in).

4   From red satin ribbon, cut 8 lengths each, 37 cm (15 in).

MAKE ME

All seam allowances are 1 cm (⅜ in).

1   To make the table runner, alternate the gingham and white cotton panels, arranging them so that the wider white cotton fabric pieces are each at the end of the table runner. With right sides, stitch the pieces together along the 37 cm (15 in) edges to form one length. Press the seams open.

2   Space the yo-yos evenly on the panels at each end of the table runner, remembering to take into account the 1 cm (½ in) seam that will be needed at each end to sew the back to the table runner front. Stitch the yo-yos in place.

3   Pin a length of satin ribbon over each seam and sew in place along both edges using matching thread.

4   Place the table runner and calico lining right sides together. Trim the lining length to match the table runner length. Sew around all edges, leaving a gap on one side for turning. Turn right side out and press. Ladder stitch the opening closed.

TIPS

Work slowly when attaching the ribbon to ensure your stitching is as straight as possible.

Use a fabric marker to mark the position of each yo-yo on the white fabric so that you don't need to keep measuring as you attach each one.

Why not make some matching placements for a complete table setting?

CHRISTMAS CUSHION

Add some festive cheer to your lounge with a few of these Christmas cushions.

SHOPPING LIST

* 105 x 46 cm (41½ x 18 in) white cotton, for the cushion front and back
* 18 cm x 46 cm (7 x 18 in) red reindeer fabric, for the panel
* 1 m (1 yd) of 5 mm (¼ in) wide red ric-rac braid
* 2 m (79 in) of red twist cord, for the cushion edging
* 51 cm (20 in) cushion insert
* Matching sewing thread

ESSENTIALS

* Sewing machine
* Iron and ironing board
* Fabric scissors
* Large hand-sewing needle
* Pins

PREPARE ME

1 From white cotton, cut 1 square, 46 cm (18 in), for the cushion front. Cut 2 rectangles, each 28 x 46 cm (11 x 18 in), for the cushion back.

2 Cut 2 lengths of red ric-rac braid, each 46 cm (18 in).

MAKE ME

All seam allowances are 1 cm (⅜ in).

1 Arrange the reindeer panel, right side up, on the right-hand side of the white cotton cushion front, placing it 6 cm (2½ in) in from the right-hand edge of the cushion front. Pin in place, then topstitch along both long edges.

2   Sew red trim along each long edge of the reindeer panel to hide the raw edges.

3   To make the cushion back, turn in a 6 mm (¼ in) hem along one long edge of each cushion back piece and press in place. Turn in the hem again to make a double hem, press, then pin and sew close to the first folded edge.

4   Place the cushion front right side up on a flat work surface. Arrange both cushion back pieces right side down so that the hemmed edges overlap at the centre. Pin in place, then sew around the edges of the cushion. Trim the seams at the corners and turn through.

DECORATE ME

1   Place the cushion insert inside the cushion cover.

2   Hand stitch the red twist cord around all edges along the seams, starting at the centre bottom and leaving a 6 cm (2½ in) unstitched tail at the beginning and end to join later.

3   Untwist the cord ends so that they lie flat, one on top of the other. Unpick the cushion seam at this point and push the ends through. Hand stitch the seam ensuring the cord twists are correct.

TIPS

Having the cushion insert inside the cushion makes it easier to hold the cushion while stitching the decorative cord in place. If you are worried that you may accidentally catch the cushion insert in the stitching then attach the cord first.

Why not make a matching set of cushions, or alternate the colourways so that you have a white reindeer panel on a red cushion?

PET BANDANA

Get the pets involved on Christmas day with this cheerful pet bandana.

SHOPPING LIST

* 45 x 30 cm (18 x 12 in) red polka dot plush fabric
* 50 x 7 cm (20 x 2¾ in) white plush fabric
* 12 x 7 cm (4¾ x 2¾ in) paper-backed fusible webbing
* 35 cm (14 in) of 5 mm (¼ in) wide red satin ribbon
* 2 skeins white embroidery thread
* Matching sewing thread

ESSENTIALS

* Sewing machine
* Iron and ironing board
* Fabric scissors
* Hand-sewing needle
* A3 printer/photocopier
* Cardboard (card stock)
* Tracing paper or template plastic
* Pencil
* Paper scissors
* Craft glue
* Baking paper

PREPARE ME

1   Trace or photocopy the pet bandana template provided and cut out.

2   Trace or photocopy the bone template provided and cut out.

3   Trace or photocopy the pom pom template twice and cut out. Glue each to cardboard and cut out.

4   From the red polka dot plush fabric, cut 2 bandanas.

5   Protecting the iron and ironing board with baking paper, iron the fusible webbing to the wrong side of

one end of the white plush fabric. Leave to cool. Draw around the bone template on the paper side of the fusible webbing, then cut out.

6   Cut 1 length of red ribbon to 3.5 cm (1½ in).

DECORATE ME

1   Remove the backing paper from the bone, then centre the motif 4 cm (1½ in) from the top of one red triangle. Press to fuse in place. Stitch over the raw edges of the bone using machine zigzag stitch.

2   Place the short piece of ribbon across the width of the bone at one side and sew along each short edge. Tie the remaining ribbon into a bow and hand stitch to the centre of the red ribbon using invisible stitches.

MAKE ME

All seam allowances are 1 cm (⅜ in).

1   Place the pet bandana pieces right sides together. Sew around all sides, using a long running stitch and leaving a small gap in the top edge for turning. Turn through and press. Ladder stitch the gap closed.

2   Fold the remaining white plush fabric in half lengthwise, with right sides together. Sew along the long raw edge to make a tube. Turn through and press.

3   Ladder stitch the sewn long edge to the top of the bandana by stitching through the seams of each.

4   To make a pom pom, place the cardboard circles together. Trim a 20 cm (8 in) length of the white

embroidery thread and set it aside for later. Wrap the cardboard circles with both skeins of the white embroidery thread. The centre hole will be extremely small when both skeins are used up (use a needle to push the thread through).

5   Holding the threads firmly at the centre of the circles, cut the edge of the wrapped thread by inserting the scissors through the thread and between each cardboard template at the outer edge.

6   Tie the 20 cm (8 in) leftover thread around the centre between the cardboard templates, leaving two long tails for attaching to the bandana. Carefully remove the templates and fluff out the threads to create a round pom pom.

7   Thread the pom pom tails through the point of the bandana, pulling tightly so that there is no excess thread between the edge of the pom pom and the bandana. Knot and trim the thread ends.

8   Thread the pet's collar through the white plush fabric tube.

TIPS

Rolling the finished pom pom between your hands can help even out the threads. Clip any ends that are longer than the rest.

To make a bandana suitable for a cat, change the appliqué design and make the bandana smaller.

Simply thread your pet's collar through the ends of the white plush tube and secure around your pet's neck.

GOODY POCKET BUNTING

An alternative to an advent calender, this pocket bunting can be filled with themed sweet treats, messages, components of a project such as beads, or candy.

SHOPPING LIST

- 80 x 35 cm (31½ x 14 in) cream fabric, for the pockets
- 40 x 11 cm (16 x 4½ in) decorative green cotton fabric, for the pocket decoration
- 30 x 11 cm (12 x 4½ in) red snowflake cotton fabric, for the pocket decoration
- 1.5 m x 5 cm (60 x 2 in) red cotton fabric or bias binding, for the binding strip
- Sewing thread to match

ESSENTIALS

- Sewing machine
- Iron and ironing board
- Fabric scissors
- Tape measure
- Pins

PREPARE ME

1   From cream fabric, cut 7 rectangles each 21.5 x 11 cm (8½ x 4½ in), for the pocket fronts. Cut 7 rectangles each 12 x 11 cm (4¾ x 4½ in) for the pocket backing.

2   From decorative green cotton, cut 4 rectangles each 10 x 11 cm (4 x 4½ in), for the pocket decoration.

3   From red snowflake cotton, cut 3 rectangles each 10 x 11 cm (4 x 4½ in), for the pocket decoration.

MAKE ME

All seam allowances are 1 cm (⅜ in).

1   Fold each decorative rectangle in half lengthwise, wrong sides together. Place on the wrong side of one pocket front, matching 11 cm (4½ in) raw edges. Stitch the pocket decoration in place on the short edge. Flip the decoration to the right side and press.

2   Fold the pocket front, wrong sides together, so that the top of the decorative edge sits 4 cm (1½ in) below the other short edge.

3   Place a pocket backing on top. Adjust the pocket beneath so that both pieces are the same size and all raw edges align. Sew around all edges except for the top. Trim the seams at the corners and turn right side out. Press.

4   Fold the red binding strip in half lengthwise. Press.

5   Unfold, and turn in 5 mm (¼ in) at the short ends. Press. Fold the long raw edges in so that they meet at the centre crease. Press.

6   Fold the strip in half lengthwise so the folded edges meet and the raw edges are enclosed. Press.

7   Find the centre of the strip and insert a bunting pocket inside the strip at that point. Pin in place.

8   Space the pockets 3 cm (1¼ in) apart and continue to add pockets on each side until all 7 are pinned in place.

9   Sew along the long edge of the bunting strip where the folded edges meet, catching each bunting pocket along the way.

DECORATE ME

1   Add any decorative elements to the design to personalise it.

2   Fill each pocket with goodies.

CHRISTMAS TOTE

A seasonal tote is just the thing to carry all those Christmas gifts home from the shops.

SHOPPING LIST

* 110 x 50 cm (44 x 20 in) cream cotton fabric, for the bag outer
* 110 x 65 cm (44 x 26 in) gingham floral fabric, for the bag inner
* 20 cm (8 in) of 1 cm (⅜ in) wide gingham ribbon, tied into a bow

ESSENTIALS

* Sewing machine
* Iron and ironing board
* Fabric scissors
* Hand-sewing needle
* Fabric marker
* Tape measure
* Pins

PREPARE ME

1 From cream cotton fabric, cut 2 rectangles each 50 x 45.5 cm (20 x 18 in), for the outer bag. Cut 2 handles each 50 x 5 cm (20 x 2 in).

2 From gingham floral fabric, cut 2 rectangles, each 50 cm x 45.5 cm (20 x 18 in), for the lining. Cut 2 strips, each 7.5 x 45.5 cm (3 x 18 in), for the decorative panel at the base of the bag. Cut 3 strips, each 7.5 x 56 cm (3 x 22 in), for the ruffle at the top of the bag.

MAKE ME

All seam allowances are 1 cm (⅜ in).

1 For the decorative panel, arrange each gingham panel on a cream outer bag piece, 12.5 cm (5 in) from one shorter end. Pin and stitch in place. Machine zigzag over the raw edge.

2 Place the outer bag pieces right sides together, decorative panel aligned, and sew along the long sides and bag bottom.

3 To create a bag base, splay out the fabric at one side

seam so that the seam is aligned with that of the bag base seam and you have a pointed corner. Measure 8 cm (3¼ in) from the point along the side seam. Draw a line perpendicular to the seam at this point. Pin. Sew along the drawn line and cut away the excess seam allowance (the pointed corner). Repeat for the remaining corner. Turn the bag right side out.

4   Repeat to make the gingham lining, but this time, leave an 8 cm (3 ¼ in) gap in one long side for turning through.

5   Place the outer bag inside the lining so that the right sides are facing.

6   To make the ruffle, sew the 7.5 x 56 cm (3 x 22 in) strips of gingham together at the short ends to create one long circular strip. Fold the strip in half lengthwise, wrong sides together, and press. Make a gathering stitch close to the raw edges, leaving a long tail at the start and finish.

7   Divide the ruffle into quarters and mark each quarter point with a pin. Position the ruffle between the bag outer and lining, raw edges aligned, matching the pins marking the quarter points with the side seams and the halfway points between the seams. Pull up the gathering stitches so that the ruffle fits to the bag outer between the seams and the gathers are evenly distributed around the bag.

8   To make the handles, fold one cream handle in half lengthwise and press. Unfold, then fold the long raw edges in so they meet at the centre crease. Press. Fold the strip in half lengthwise so the folded edges meet and the raw edges are enclosed. Press. Sew down the long edge where the folded edges meet. Repeat for other handle.

9   Place one handle between the outer bag and the lining so that handles are inside the bag and the raw edges are matching at the top edge. Each handle end should be 12 cm (4¾ in) in from a side seam. Pin in place. Pin all layers together by removing the ruffle pins one at a time and pushing the pins through all layers.

10 Sew around the top of the bag through all layers. Turn the bag right side out through the gap in the lining and push the lining into the bag. The ruffle should sit proud at the top of the bag. Ladder stitch the gap in the lining closed. Press the bag.

DECORATE ME

1   Hand stitch the gingham bow to the centre front of one gingham decorative panel.

SNOWMAN GIFT BAG

Make someone's day with this adorable little gift bag.

SHOPPING LIST

* 10 cm (4 in) thin cream cord, for the loops to hold the scarf in place
* 8 x 48 cm (3½ x 19 in) red polka dot fabric, for the scarf
* 12 x 40 cm (5 x 16 in) cream cotton fabric, for the bag outer
* 12 x 40 cm (5 x 16 in) white cotton fabric decorated with red polka dots, for the bag lining
* 2 small red buttons, for eyes
* 3 polka dot buttons, for decoration

* Black embroidery thread, for the mouth
* Orange embroidery thread, for the nose
* Matching sewing thread
* Toy stuffing (optional)

ESSENTIALS

* Sewing machine
* Iron and ironing board
* Small hand-sewing needle
* Large hand-sewing needle
* Fabric scissors
* Erasable fabric marker

PREPARE ME

1 Cut the thin cream cord into two equal lengths.

2 To make the scarf, fold the red polka dot fabric in half lengthwise, wrong sides together, and press. Open out the fold, then turn in 5mm (¼ in) at each short end. Press. Turn in the long edges to meet at the centre crease. Press. Fold in half lengthwise and press. Stitch in place where the folded edges meet.

MAKE ME

All seam allowances are 1 cm (⅜ in).

1   Fold the cream cotton bag outer in half, right sides together, so the short ends meet. With the short raw ends at the top, mark a point down each side, 7 cm (2¾ in) from the top and another 9 cm (3½ in) from the top. Insert each short length of cord between the two layers of fabric so that each end of each cord will be caught in the stitching at the marked points. These create 'belt' loops for the scarf so only the ends are within the seam. (There is extra length added to the cord here for ease of handling). Sew along both long edges, catching in each end of the cord only at each mark on each side. Sew over the cord ends 3 or 4 times for added strength, then trim the ends. Turn the bag right side out and tease out the corners.

2   Fold the lining fabric, right sides together, so the short ends meet. Sew along both long edges, leaving a 4 cm (1½ in) gap on one side for turning.

DECORATE ME

1   Sew the polka dot buttons to the outer bag front, placing the first button 3 cm (1¼ in) from the bag bottom and the other two each 2.5 cm (1 in) apart.

2   Sew 2 red buttons on for eyes, positioning them 2 cm (¾ in) from the bag top and 3 cm (1¼ in) from the sides.

3   Hand stitch a 1.5 cm (½ in) long carrot nose.

4   Hand stitch 6 black crosses for the mouth.

5   Place the bag outer inside the bag lining, with right sides together and top raw edges aligned. Sew around the bag top and turn through the gap in the lining. Close the gap in the lining using ladder stitch. Push the lining into the bag. Press carefully.

6   Thread the scarf through the loops and tie at one side.

TIPS

Use different fabrics to create a unique bag for each recipient.
Trim the excess fabric from the corners before turning to help create sharp points when pushing out.
Put a little toy stuffing in with your treats to give your snowman a round belly.
Fill the snowman bag with Christmas treats.

ADVENT CALENDAR

This sweet Christmas house advent calendar is perfect for the count down to Christmas day.

SHOPPING LIST

* 90 x 35 cm (36 x 14 in) white felt, for the house
* 65 x 15 cm (26 x 6 in) red felt, for the pockets and heart
* 1 spool of 1 cm (⅜ in) wide red and white heart ribbon
* 10 cm (4 in) of 1 cm (⅜ in) wide red satin ribbon, for the hanging loop
* 1.5 m (60 in) of 5 mm (¼ in) wide white ric-rac braid
* 20 cm (8 in) of 1 cm (⅜ in) wide white organza ribbon
* Matching sewing thread

ESSENTIALS

* Sewing machine
* Fabric scissors
* Paper scissors
* Hand-sewing needle
* Fabric marker or pen
* Craft glue
* Paper
* A4 printer
* Tape measure
* Computer and printer
* Light box

PREPARE ME

1   From the white felt, cut 1 rectangle 58.5 x 32 cm (23 x 12¾ in). One 32 cm (12¾ in) edge is the top of the calendar. Mark the centre of the top edge. Mark 11 cm (4¼ in) from the top edge on each side edge. Join each side mark to the centre top mark to create a point. Cut along both lines to create the roof of the house.

2   From the red felt, cut 24 rectangles, each 5 x 5.5 cm (2 x 2¼ in). Using the template provided for the Christmas Tree Heart project, cut one heart.

3   Type the digits 1 to 24 using a sans serif font in word processing software. I used the typeface Arial, and made the digits bold and size 100. Print the

numbers. Place the numbers on a light source such as a window or computer or tablet screen, and place a remnant of the white felt on top. Trace the numbers using a fabric marker or pen, spacing them out so you have sufficient room to manoeuvre when cutting out the digits. Cut out each number, ensuring there is no ink visible at the edges. Set side.

4   Cut 4 lengths of heart ribbon to the length of the roof slope. Cut 1 length of heart ribbon to the length of the house base.

MAKE ME

1   Bring the short ends of the red satin ribbon together to create a hanging loop. Position behind the point of the roof. Sew in place (the heart ribbon will cover this stitching).

2   Arrange the red felt pockets on the house, positioning them 4 cm (1½ in) below the roof slope and arranging them in six rows so that there is 2 cm (¾ in) between rows and 1.5 cm (½ in) between columns. When you are happy with the arrangement, pin each in place, then stitch the sides and base of each pocket to the house background.

3   Glue a number to each square, arranging them in numerical order.

DECORATE ME

1   Glue the heart to the centre of the roof area. Tie the white organza ribbon into a bow. Glue to the centre top of the heart.

2   Glue 2 heart ribbon lengths next to each other on each side of the roof.

3   Glue 1 heart ribbon length to the base of the house.

4   Cut a piece of white ric-rac braid to fit the width of each square, then glue one length to the top of each square.

TIPS

If you use a red pen to trace the letters, it isn't noticeable if some ink is left on the letters because the background is also red.
It helps to place a weight on top of the bow while the glue is drying.

THE 12 DAYS OF CHRISTMAS ADVENT CALENDAR

For something different, try this 12 Days of Christmas Advent Calendar. Test a loved one on what each day represents in the well-known song of the same name and reward correct guesses with a treat. I've included instructions for covering a corkboard to serve as a base for the advent calendar hearts.

SHOPPING LIST

* 35 x 15 cm (14 x 6 in) pink pin dot fabric, for the hearts
* 35 x 15 cm (14 x 6 in) blue floral fabric, for the hearts
* 20 cm (8 in) square of white hessian (burlap), for the hearts and the circles on which the numbers are embroidered
* Calico (enough to cover the corkboard) (optional)
* Batting (wadding) (enough to cover the corkboard) (optional)
* Toy stuffing
* Dark pink embroidery thread
* Light pink embroidery thread
* Matching sewing thread
* Corkboard and 12 push pins (optional)
* 25 cm (10 in) of 1 cm (⅜ in) wide ribbon

ESSENTIALS

* Sewing machine
* Fabric scissors
* Large hand-sewing needle
* Fabric marker
* Craft glue
* Scrap piece of heavyweight cardboard
* A4 photocopier (optional)
* Tracing paper or template plastic (optional)
* Paper scissors (optional)
* Pencil (optional)
* Accuquilt Go! Baby (optional)
* Accuquilt Go! Heart 5 cm, 7,5 cm, 10 cm (2 in, 3 in, 4 in) cutting die (optional)
* Accuquilt Go! cutting mat (optional)

PREPARE ME

1   If you are not using the Go! Baby, photocopy or trace the heart template provided for the Christmas Tree Heart project. Glue the copy to cardboard and cut out.

2   Draw 12 circles, each 2.5 cm (1 in) in diameter, on the hessian.

3   Use a pen or fabric marker to draw numbers 1 to 12 inside the circles. These will be embroidered in a later step.

4   If you are using the Go! Baby, cut a strip of blue fabric wide enough to cover the largest Go! Baby heart on the cutting die and from selvedge to selvedge.

5   Layer the strips over the largest heart to get as many hearts as possible from the strips. Place cutting mat on top and roll through the Go! Baby.

6   Once cut, the scraps surrounding the heart should provide some half hearts that are perfect to use for the back pockets. Snip excess fabric away from these half hearts so they are ready to use.

7   Repeat Steps 3–5 until you have 11 blue hearts and 5 blue half hearts (the half hearts don't need to be exactly the same size – some will be a bit smaller than others) and repeat steps 3–5 with the pink fabric until you have 11 pink hearts and 7 pink half hearts. If you are not using the Go! Baby, use the heart template as a guide and cut out the required number of hearts and half hearts. Repeat Steps 3–5 to cut 2 hearts from the white hessian.

8   Place the batting on the calico fabric and cut the calico 2 cm (¾ in) larger on each side than the batting.

MAKE ME

All seam allowances are 5 mm (¼ in) (except corkboard cover)

OPTIONAL CORKBOARD

1   If you'd like to make the corkboard, place glue on the edges of the batting and fold the seam allowance of the white calico fabric over onto the batting, pressing down to glue in place. Check that the piece now fits over the cork of the corkboard and within the frame. Adjust size if necessary.

2   Place glue on the edges and in the centre area of the cork on the corkboard. Press the calico/ batting piece onto the glue to secure.

HEARTS

1   Pair up the hearts so that each pair has one full heart of each colour and one half heart of the front colour (for example, if a heart has a blue front and a pink back, the half heart should be blue).

2   Turn in a tiny hem on the straight edge of each half heart and stitch in place.

3   Place each full heart pair right sides together with a half heart in between. Start sewing around the edges of each pair, starting on the right hand side, 1 cm (½ in) from the base, and ending on the same side just after the top of the half heart.

4   Trim the point and clip the seam allowance (but do not cut through the seam) around the curves at the centre top point. Turn the heart right side out, so the half heart is also right side out. Press.

5   Thread a piece of embroidery thread through the gap in the side and up through the centre top of the heart. Thread back down on the other side of the centre stitch and through the gap in the side. Trim the ends at the gap, ensuring a tiny loop is poking out of the top. Tie a double knot in the ends and then pull the loop up. Alternate between dark and light pink embroidery thread for each heart.

6   Embroider over the drawn numbers on the hessian and cut out the circle that contains each.

7   Insert the cardboard strip that was used to draw the circles in between the two layers of the heart (see Tips).

8   Using matching pink sewing thread, sew around the number to attach the circle to the front of the heart. The cardboard will ensure the needle doesn't catch the back heart when stitching—simply move it around as you go.

9   Stuff the heart firmly with hobby fill and ladder stitch the opening closed.

10 When making the hessian heart, use a blue back and ensure to stay stitch the opening to prevent fraying.

DECORATE ME

1   Form the pin dot ribbon into a bow and stitch to the white hessian heart.

2   If using the covered pin board, push the pins into the covered corkboard, making sure to space them evenly. Hang the hearts on each pin so colours alternate and numbers are in order.

3   Alternatively, you can use any pin board or hang these up wherever you like—on a Christmas tree, over the mantel piece, along a staircase banister—it's up to you!

TIPS

To create a circle of a particular diameter, cut a small piece of cardboard (card stock) 1 cm (½ in) wide and slightly longer than the radius of your circle. Mark two points along the cardboard piece that have a distance between them that equals the radius measurement. Poke a hole at each mark (one will need to be large enough to fit the end of a pencil or fabric marker through). Put the end of your unpicker in one hole and onto the fabric. Put the end of your marker in the other hole and onto the fabric. Then, simply move the marker in a circle around the unpicker to draw a perfect circle.

TIPS

Sew slowly when attaching the inner circle to the outer ring to ensure stitching is as neat and even as possible. The inner edge of the outer ring should be approximately 5 mm (¼ in) past the inner edge of the white binding when overlapping the two pieces.

Tie your lovely quilt around the base of your Christmas tree ready for presents.

QUILTED TREE SKIRT

When I was shopping for fabric for this project, this pink and green Christmas tree fabric really appealed to me. I love how bright it is. The dark pink surrounding the inner circle really helps the white centre to stand out.

SHOPPING LIST

* 78 cm (31 in) square Christmas tree-print fabric
* 1.5 x 1.1 m (60 x 44 in) pink reindeer fabric
* 78 cm (31 in) square batting (wadding)
* 2.5 x 1.1 m (100 x 44 in) white cotton fabric, for binding and lining
* Matching sewing thread

ESSENTIALS

* Sewing machine
* Fabric scissors
* Hand-sewing needle
* Unpicker
* Fabric marker
* Pattern-making paper
* Paper scissors
* Pencil
* Ruler and tape measure
* Iron and ironing board

PREPARE ME

1   Starting at one end, mark the following points along the length of the cardboard strip: 2 cm (¾ in), 7 cm (2¾ in), 39 cm (15½ in), 41 cm (16¼ in), 51 cm (20 in). Make holes at all points.

2   Place the cardboard strip on the pattern paper so that the 2 cm (¾ in) hole is at the centre of the paper.

3   Push the end of an unpicker into the 2 cm (¾ in) hole (keeping it in the centre of the paper) and a sharp pencil into the 41 cm (16¼ in) hole. Drag the pencil in a circle to draw a 78 cm (31 in) diameter circle, as if you are using a compass.

4   Keeping the unpicker in the centre, move the pencil to the 7 cm (2¾ in) hole. Draw a circle by dragging the pencil around the centre. This will create a 10 cm (4 in) diameter circle. This creates the inner circle pattern.

5   To make the outer ring pattern, which is one-quarter of the full ring. Move to another part of the paper where you can draw this without overlapping the 78 cm (31 in) circle pattern piece. Push the end of the unpicker into the 2 cm (¾ in) hole and a sharp pencil into the 41 cm (16 ¼ in) hole. Draw a quarter circle, which should be exactly one-quarter of the 78 cm (31 in) circle plus 2 cm (¾ in) at each end for seam allowance.

6   Move the pencil to the 39 cm (15 ½ in) hole and draw another quarter-circle line next to the first one (do not change the position of the unpicker).

7   Move the pencil to the 51 cm (20 in) hole and draw another quarter circle line (again, do not change the position of the unpicker).

8   Draw a perpendicular line at each end by joining the ends of the 39 cm (15½ in) and 51 cm (20 in) lines. You should now have a quarter ring pattern that is 12 cm (4½ in) wide and includes 2 cm (¾ in) of seam allowance on the inner curve and at each end.

9   Cut out both pattern pieces on the outer lines and fold the quarter ring in half so the short ends meet.

10 Cut out the inner circle from the 78 cm (31 in) circle.

11 Fold the pink reindeer fabric in half lengthwise,

right sides together. Place the fold of the quarter ring pattern on the fold of the fabric. Pin around all edges. Cut around the pattern piece. Repeat 3 more times to create four full-quarter rings (ensure the direction of the reindeer pattern is correct on all pieces)

12 Repeat with the white fabric for the outer ring backing.

13 Arrange the white tree fabric wrong side up and pin the 78 cm (31 in) circle to it. Pin. Cut around the pattern piece. Do not cut out the inner circle.

14 Repeat step 13 with the batting and the white fabric.

15 Cut two strips on the bias from the reindeer fabric, 5 x 67.5 cm (2 x 26½ in), for the inner binding.

16 Cut four strips from the reindeer fabric, 6 x 56 cm (2¼ x 22 in), for the bows.

17 Cut four strips on the bias, 65 x 6.5 cm (25½ x 2½ in) from the white fabric, for the outer binding.

MAKE ME

Use a 1 cm (⅜ in) seam allowance.

1   Place the 78 cm (31 in) white cotton lining circle on the work surface. Put the batting on top and then the Christmas tree fabric, right side up on top. Pin the layers together every 6 cm (2½ in) all across the circle. Sew around the outer edge of the circle, through all layers, 5 mm (¼ in) from the edge.

2   Flip the circle so that the white lining is facing

up. Arrange the paper pattern on top. Using a fabric marker, draw the inner circle on the white fabric. Using a ruler, draw a straight line on the white lining joining the inner and outer circles.

3   Sew 5 mm (¼ in) outside the inner circle and on both sides of the straight line. Cut on the straight drawn line and around the inner circle line. Machine quilt around the outside of each tree of the printed fabric.

4   Join the white binding strips to make one long length. Press open the seams. Fold in half lengthwise and press. Open out the fold. Fold each long edge in to the centre fold and press. Press in half again. Open out the binding. Pin one long raw edge to the Christmas tree side of the quilted skirt, matching raw edges. Sew along the first fold. Flip the binding to the lining side, turning under the raw edge and slipstitch in place. Trim the ends to match the ends of the tree skirt. Repeat to create an binding strip using reindeer fabric and use to bind the inner circle.

5   Place the reindeer underskirt pieces around the quilted circle and pin in place to check the size. Unpin and trim to fit. Pin the short ends right sides together, then sew the 4 pieces together, but do not join the the final seam at the back of the circle. Repeat with the lining.

6   Place the underskirt lining and reindeer fabric right sides together. Sew along the inner and outer curves. Clip the seam allowance of the inner curve, making sure you don't cut through the seam. Turn through and press.

7   Place the underskirt right side up. Arrange the quilted skirt on top (also right side up). The outer edge of the quilted skirt should overlap the underskirt and the ends should match those of the skirt. Pin in place.

8   Sew together just inside the inner edge of the white binding (do not sew on the binding), leaving 2 cm (¾ in) unstitched at each end.

9   Fold the raw edge of the outer ring in (trimming shorter if necessary) and ladder stitch the edges closed. Whipstitch the ends of the underskirt to the back of the quilted skirt, if necessary.

DECORATE ME

1   For the bows, fold the strips in half lengthwise wrong sides together, and press. Unfold and fold in the short ends by 5 mm (¼ in). Press. Fold the long edges toward the centre so they meet at the centre crease. Press. Fold the strips in half lengthwise so that the raw edges are enclosed and press. Sew along the long edge where folded edges meet.

2   Use whip stitch to attach one end of each strip to the back of the quilt. Two strips should be 7 cm (2¾ in) from the inner circle edge and two strips should be 7 cm (2¾ in) from the outer edge. Tie the strips into bows.

TEMPLATES

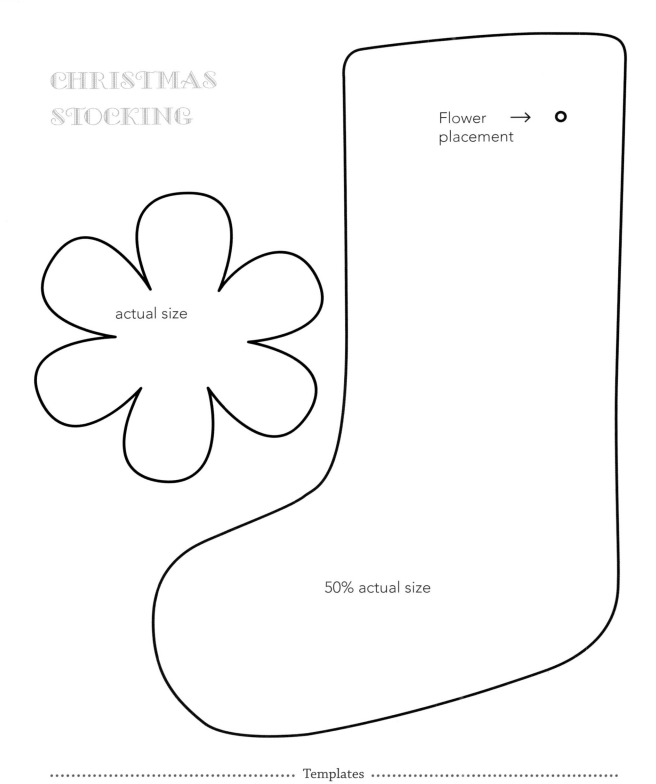

CHRISTMAS
STOCKING

Flower placement → ○

actual size

50% actual size

actual size

SANTA HAT PET BANDANA

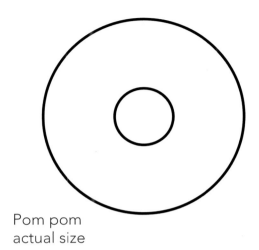

Pom pom
actual size

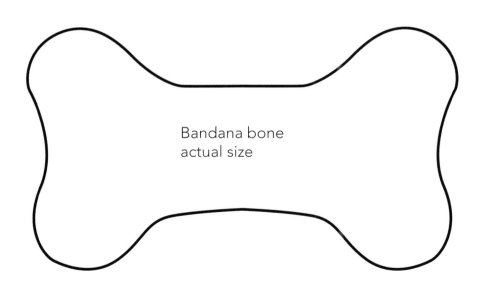

Bandana bone
actual size

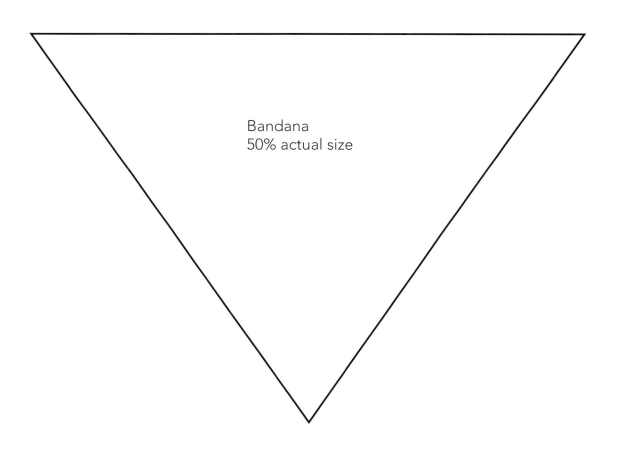

Bandana
50% actual size

Small heart
actual size

Large heart
actual size

CHRISTMAS TREE HEART

actual size

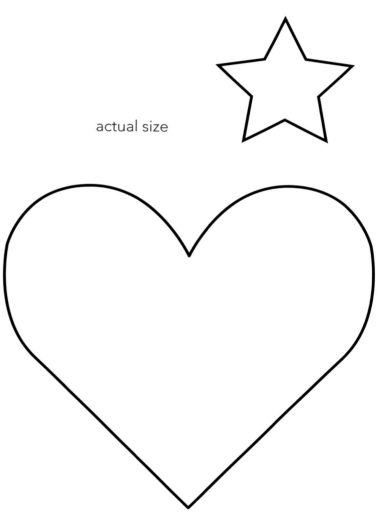

CHRISTMAS TREE REINDEER

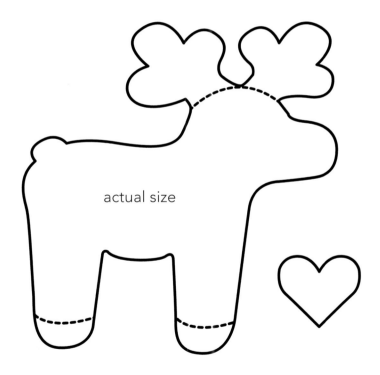

actual size

CHRISTMAS TREE STAR

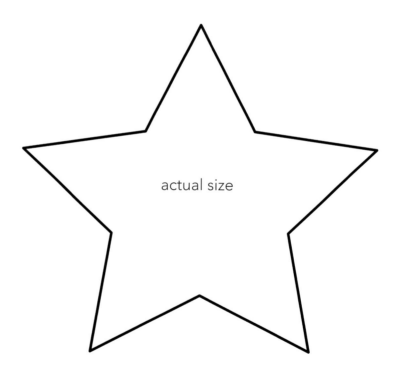

actual size

TINY CHRISTMAS TREE STOCKING

actual size

Yo-yo 11 cm (4⅛ in) circle

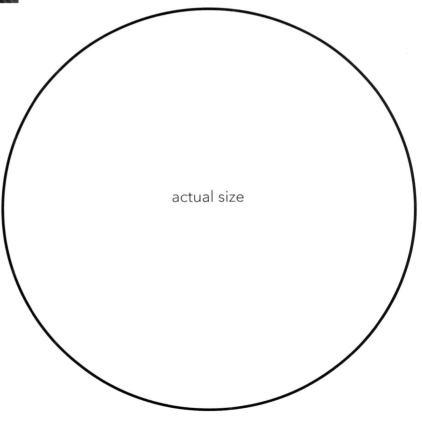

actual size

NOEL BUNTING

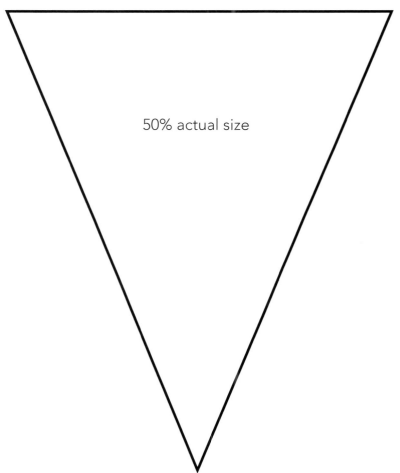

50% actual size

actual size

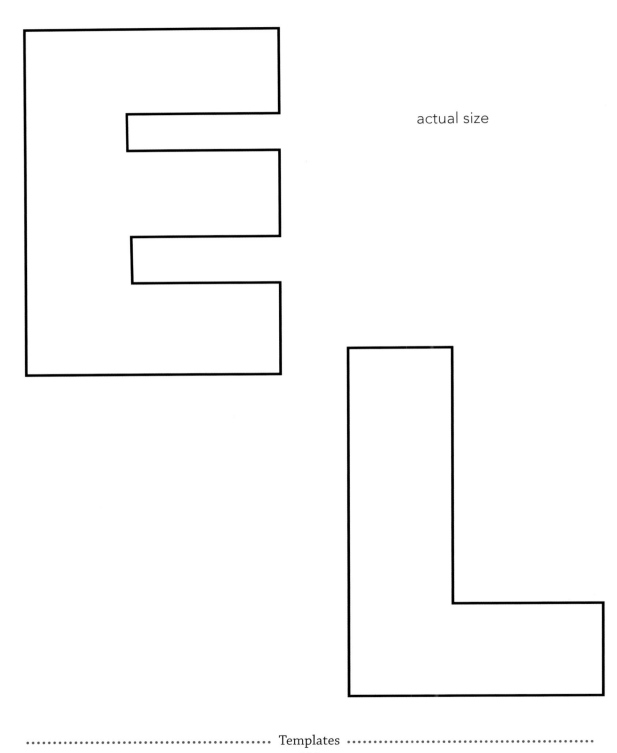

actual size

BASIC BUNTING

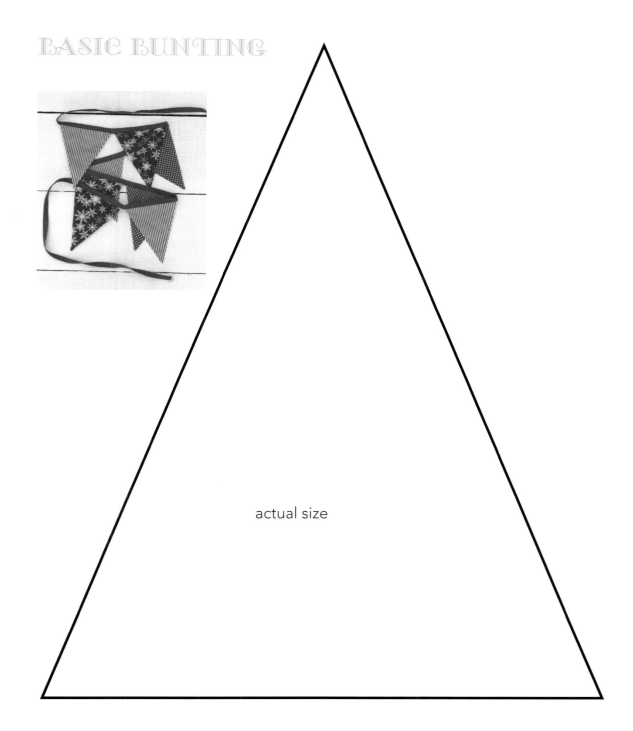

actual size

First published in 2014 by New Holland Publishers Pty Ltd
London • Sydney • Auckland

The Chandlery Unit 704 50 Westminster Bridge Road London SE1 7QY United Kingdom
1/66 Gibbes Street Chatswood NSW 2067 Australia
5/39 Woodside Ave Northcote Auckland 0627 New Zealand

www.newhollandpublishers.com

A record of this book is held at the British Library and the National Library of Australia.

ISBN 9781742575940

Managing director: Fiona Schultz
Publisher: Diane Ward
Editor: Simona Hill
Designer: Lorena Susak
Photographs: Samantha Mackie
Production Director: Olga Dementiev
Printer: Toppan Leefung Printing Ltd

10 9 8 7 6 5 4 3

Keep up with New Holland Publishers on Facebook
www.facebook.com/NewHollandPublishers